Sr Jude Groden RS

Corinn...
Tony C...
Dawn...
Colette...

With a foreword by Dr Jack Dominian

A Journey in LOVE

A developmental programme for children in the primary years

McCrimmons   Great Wakering   Essex

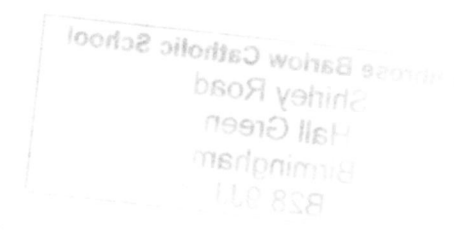

First published in United Kingdom in 2006 by
MCCRIMMON PUBLISHING CO LTD
10-12 High Street, Great Wakering, Essex SS3 0EQ
Telephone 01702-218956   Fax 01702-216082
Email: info@mccrimmons.com
Website: www.mccrimmons.com

© 2005/2006 Sr Jude Groden

ISBN 0 85597 684 5   (10 digit ISBN)
ISBN 978-0-85597-684-2   (13 digit ISBN)
McCrimmon order ref: MB6845

Narrative text: Sr Jude Groden

Illustrations: Gunvor Edwards

Nihil Obstat	Mgr. George Stokes. Censor Deputatus
Imprimatur	+Thomas McMahon, Bishop of Brentwood.

ACKNOWLEDGEMENTS
Extracts from RELATIONSHIPS IN MORAL EDUCATION (draft document), Michael McGrath, Catholic Education Commission, Scotland 2000. Used by permission.

ISBN 0 85597 684 5

Design and layout by Nick Snode
Layout assistance by Tania Dauptain
Typeset in ITC Eras and Trebuchet
Printed and bound by Geerings Print, Ashford, Kent, UK / www.geeringsprint.co.uk

J/AG

Contents

	FOREWORD	4
	A VISION STATEMENT	5
	INTRODUCTION	6
N	NURSERY Wonder at God's Love	7
R	RECEPTION YEAR God loves each of us in our uniqueness	11
1	YEAR ONE We meet God's love in our family	15
2	YEAR TWO We meet God's love in the community	19
3	YEAR THREE How we live in love	23
4	YEAR FOUR God loves us in our differences	28
5	YEAR FIVE God loves me in my changing and development	33
6	YEAR SIX The wonder of God's love in creating new life	38
	JOURNEY OF LIFE	46
	SOME PERSPECTIVES ON MARRIAGE	47
	GLOSSARY	50

Foreword

AT THE HEART of Christian faith is love, St John says that God is love (1 John 4:8) and the whole purpose of Christianity is to live it as fully as possible in and through love. This means we have to link every aspect of our being, from birth to death, with love.

Love starts to enter our life the moment of birth when we are held tenderly in the arms of our mother and developed throughout our first intimate relationship of childhood with our parents, family members, friends and teachers. At puberty the secondary sexual characteristics arise. Now we begin to seek someone from outside our family and, armed with our first relationship, we explore our second intimate relationship of love usually ending in marriage.

The whole purpose of education at home, in the primary school is to connect every aspect of growth, physical, emotional, intellectual and social with love. The ultimate goal is to enable adults to fully love themselves i.e. accept themselves positively, and in turn able to love their neighbour i.e. make themselves fully available to others.

The alliance of the fullness of ourselves with love links us with God the Father, through Jesus Christ his Son, and through the Spirit. Jesus accepted himself totally in the Incarnation and made himself fully available to the world and to each and everyone of us, especially on the Cross, the pinnacle of his love.

Parents and teachers are privileged to assist children every moment of their lives to further this link of love with their humanity and thus with God. The programme outlined in a Journey in Love is a brilliant reconciliation between the human and divine aspects of love and is truly fully Christian in its vision.

This vision is none other than the Kingdom of God, summed up by Jesus in the double commandments of loving God and our neighbour as ourselves. In its realisation the teacher in the primary education has a necessary and vital role to play.

Dr. Jack Dominian

A vision statement

TO BE MADE in the image of God means to be a person in relationship. It is in this context that our sexuality grows and develops from the moment of our conception. From early childhood we are on a journey of exploration of the richness various patterns of relationship offer and the appropriate tokens of exchange that they demand or admit.

In childhood, we love, we hate, we play, we fight and within all this we discover that selfishness and an unwillingness to share, not only those things precious to us, but something of ourselves, brings loneliness and bitterness. Isolation robs us of self-knowledge and a sense of fulfilment. Within this journey of exploration is God Himself, Who is Trinity – Father, Son and Holy Spirit – One God, Who is Love and Love is the highest form of relationship. So God is at the heart of love. He is at the heart of our family ties and our friendships. He reveals Himself through our pattern of interdependence. And all our interdependences operate from our sexuality.

As puberty advances we become more aware of ourselves as sexual beings and some of the relationships we share become more emotionally charged. We need to find new and appropriate expressions for them. This can be a very confusing time, but even in the confusion, God is there. The young person is exploring the whole business of belonging, being part of, identifying with others. For many, this will be the first experience of "falling in love". New tokens of exchange require to be found, new means of expression are sought, and as this search continues, there is a growing awareness that none are really satisfying, none bring that sense of fulfilment and completeness. The young person needs these experiences of the joy of beginning and the heartbreak of ending such highly charged relationships and, for many, they form the foundation for that life-long commitment to another in marriage.

The discovery of the right partner for life is like discovering "bone of my bone and flesh of my flesh" as the Book of Genesis has it, and as this relationship grows so grows also the desire to commit one's whole being to the other. The Sacrament of Marriage declares the commitment of each spouse to the other permanently in the acknowledgement that it is God-given. The sexuality of each complements the other's. In sexual union, husband and wife offer themselves selflessly to one another in the deepest expression of love possible and in that act the Sacrament is made real; each experience the depth of God's love.

Mgr. George Stokes

Introduction

> 'God's love for us is fundamental for our lives, and it raises important questions about who God is and who we are.'
>
> Deus Caritas Est 2

THIS TEACHERS' RESOURCE, A Journey in Love, has as its foundational premise the belief that we are made in the image and likeness of God and, as a consequence, gender and sexuality are God's gift, reflect God's beauty and share in the divine creativity.

In order that children may grow and develop healthily and holistically towards an understanding of their gender and its implications for successful relationships, they must be at ease with themselves and grow in self-knowledge.

An aspect of the mystery of love is treated in each year group; children and young people are encouraged to marvel at the wonder and beauty of God's creative love. This is reflected in each stage of a person's growth in the Primary years through a series of suggested, progressive and developmental tasks, activities and reflections which focus on physical, social, emotional, intellectual and spiritual development.

This text is the result of much study, discussion and shared reflection. It was a very talented team with interdisciplinary skills, drawing upon the diverse experience of educators, in consultation with parents and different experts in various fields: Corinne Adams, Tony Castle, Dawn Collis, Colette Dawson, Delia Doyle, Imelda Gunn, Katrina Karwacinski and Bozena Laraway.

I am extremely grateful to all who have collaborated in the production of this script, sponsored by Brentwood Religious Education Service. It is enriched by the artwork of Gunver Edwards and the foreword by Dr Jack Dominian.

The team of compilers is greatly assured that this resource does not contradict Catholic teaching and we are therefore, most grateful for the canonical permission given by Bishop Thomas McMahon after consultation with Monsignor George Stokes.

Sr Jude Groden RSM
PRIMARY R.E. ADVISER

> 'Love is the light – and in the end, the only light – that can always illuminate a world grown dim and give us the courage needed to keep living and working.
> Love is possible, and we are able to practise it because we are created in the image of God.'
>
> Deus Caritas Est 39

NURSERY

Wonder at God's love

PHYSICAL

(1) Children focus on their hands e.g. size, length of fingers, nails.

(2) Children focus on each others eyes and note colour and shape.

(3) Children focus on their faces and whole body shapes, size, shape, features.

LEARNING OBJECTIVES

Children begin to know and understand that they are part of the wonder of God's love and creation

ACTIVITIES

- Children draw round their hands, decorate and display in circle, dove, tree, flower, shapes etc.

- Children look at themselves in the mirror and concentrate on their own eyes – colour, shape etc.

- Look at the faces of other children. Look in the mirror at own face, note shape, size, colour, lips, nose, etc.

- Draw themselves using the correct colour for skin and features (using people pencils) and display.

PAUSE and REFLECT

Music – drawings placed in circle shape on carpet and all sing 'WE ARE SPECIAL'.

PRAYER

*Loving God,
thank you for the wonder of me.
Amen.*

KEYWORDS
*God
Wonder
Love
Creation
Hands
Fingers
Nails
Faces
Noses
Lips
Ears
Hair
Features
Colour
Shape
Size*

NURSERY

A Journey in Love

SOCIAL

(1) Children look at the pictures from previous session. Do they all look the same? Reinforce that all pictures disclose difference but each one is special.

(2) How many boys and girls in the class?

(3) Divide children into groups for a play activity.

SKILLS
Listening
Observing
Praying
Relating

ACTIVITIES

- Encourage children to share their observances, e.g. are they happy with the pictures of themselves/their friends?
- All children, boys and girls are friends together.
- Group activities to music, e.g. clap/stamp/jump etc. Taking turns to observe each other.

PAUSE and REFLECT

All children sing:
'HEADS, SHOULDERS, KNEES AND TOES.'

Assemble quietly on carpet and pray.

PRAYER

Loving God,
thank you for all that I can do
Amen.

EMOTIONAL

(1) Children begin to observe and become sensitive to facial expressions.

(2) Focus on individual expression.

(3) Help children to discover the beauty of their smile.

A Journey in Love

NURSERY

ACTIVITIES

- Ask children how they feel and write/display responses with symbols, e.g. happy, sad etc.
- Use mirrors – how do I look today?
- Look in the mirror and show biggest smile to self (for as long as they like).
  Put mirrors down and show big smile to each other.
  Repeat activity with sad faces.

PAUSE and REFLECT

Music – assemble quietly on the carpet.
Think about my smiley face.
Think about my sad face.
Children hold hands and pray.

PRAYER

Loving God,
whether I am happy or sad you love me. Amen.

INTELLECTUAL

(1) Children focus on the cause of happy and sad feelings.

(2) Identify the signs of feeling happy/sad.

(3) Observe expressions in photographs/newspapers etc.

ACTIVITIES

- Go round the circle and ask each child what makes them happy and what makes them sad.
- Hide face with hands and draw apart and disclose happy/sad faces. Can the children guess how you are feeling?
  Repeat with different children.
- Discuss the signs of happiness/sadness as evidenced in pictures and television, e.g. face, body language, posture.

PAUSE and REFLECT

Music – stand in a circle and link arms in a chain of love and pray.

PRAYER

Loving God,
be close to all of us in happy times and sad times. Amen.

SPIRITUAL

(1) Children focus on the wonders of God's world, e.g. people, animals, trees, land, seas etc.

(2) Children see their special place as part of the wonder of God's creation.

(3) Read scripture text –

> You created every part of me;
> and put me together in my mother's womb.

Psalm 139:13

Sing: 'IF I WERE A BUTTERFLY'

Celebration Hymnal for Everyone no.298

PRAYER

Loving God,
you gave me my hands,
  my eyes and my hair.
You made me in love
  and with love.
I thank you that I am part
of the wonder of your creation.
Amen.

RECEPTION

God loves each of us in our uniqueness

PHYSICAL

(1) Does it matter if we are different?

(2) Look at me –
    How am I different from you?

(3) Look at you –
    How are you different from me?

ACTIVITIES

- Children close their eyes and describe themselves to the person next to them.
  Focusing on describing words.

- Children look in mirrors and describe themselves to each other. Focusing on eye colour, hair colour, etc.

- Make a picture graph of eye colours in the class.
  Repeat finger prints/hand prints.

- Count how many girls/boys are in the class.

- Present each child with his/her name.
  Why were you given your special name?

- My Daddy's name is:

- My Mummy's name is:

I grew for 9 months in my mummy's womb before I was born.

LEARNING OBJECTIVES

Children know and understand that God has made them unique and that although we are all different we are all special to him.

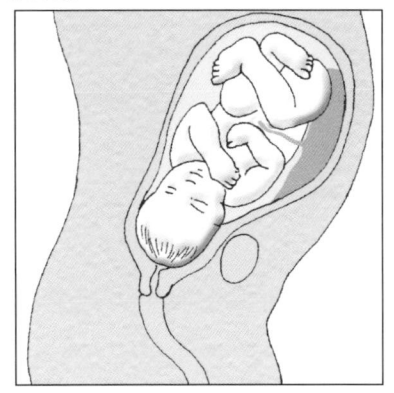

KEYWORDS

God
Unique
Different
Special
Eyes
Hair
Boy / Girl
Hands
Fingers
Name
Family
Love
Womb
Describe

RECEPTION

A Journey in Love

R

SKILLS
Listening
Observing
Relating
Speaking
Respecting
Reflecting
Praying
Understanding

PAUSE and REFLECT

Music – Candle – each child is called by name and places name around the lighted candle and all pray...

PRAYER

Loving God,
thank you for your gifts of love and for making me special
with my own name.

Amen.

SOCIAL

(1) With whom do I play with at school/home?

(2) Why does [x] play with me?

(3) Name favourite games.

ACTIVITIES

- Children pick a name from a box and name one thing that person is good at.
- List all the good qualities mentioned, e.g. *kind, helpful*

PAUSE and REFLECT

Music – assemble quietly on the carpet.

The appropriate name placed in front of each child.

Assign a 'quality' card to each pupil who places it beside name.

PRAYER

Loving God,
thank you for the gift
of my friends at home
and at school.

Amen.

A Journey in Love **RECEPTION** | 13

EMOTIONAL

(1) How do you feel about your friend?

(2) Do you both have other friends at school/home?

(3) Why do you play with them?

ACTIVITIES

- Children asked to say one thing they like about the person sitting next to them, e.g. *'you are good at...'*
- How do I show love and care for others who are not my special friends?

PAUSE and REFLECT

Music... Assemble quietly on the carpet.

Each child says in turn...

> *'I feel happy when I play with . . . .
> I feel sad when I am left out'.*

PRAYER

*Loving God,
thank you for my friends.
Help me to be a good friend
  to everyone.*

Amen.

INTELLECTUAL

(1) Is it important to have friends?

(2) Describe a good friend.

ACTIVITIES

- Read '*The Rainbow Fish*' by Marcus Pfister
- Each child makes a rainbow fish scale to create a class fish for display.
- Read and dramatise/role play '*The Good Samaritan*'.
- Talk about who was a good friend.

RECEPTION

> **PAUSE and REFLECT**
>
> Music... Assemble quietly on the carpet.
>
> Children listen to the story of the Good Samaritan and pass the Bible to each other and place in the centre and pray together.
>
> *Loving God,*
> *thank you for being my friend.*
> *Amen.*

SPIRITUAL

(1) Is Jesus our friend?

(2) Read the story 'Jesus Welcomes the Little Children' ('LISTEN' Bible p.64) and talk about children being special to God.

> **Jesus makes the children welcome**
>
> *Here is a story which shows us how much Jesus liked to meet children.*
>
> *The Reading comes from the Gospel of Saint Mark.*
>
> People often used to bring children to Jesus and when they did, Jesus always gave them his blessing.
>
> One day, however, some of the friends of Jesus told the children to go away.
>
> Jesus was angry when he saw this happening, and he said: 'Don't stop the children from coming to me. Don't send them away like that! Bring them back.'
>
> Then he put his arms round the children and he blessed them.

(3) Who is the Mother of Jesus? Why is she special?
    Jesus grew for nine months in Mary's womb.

> **PRAYER**
>
> *Loving God, we know that we are unique. Although we are different from one another*
> *we are all special to you. Amen*

A Journey in Love

YEAR ONE

We meet God's love in our family

PHYSICAL

(1) Who is in my family?
   eg. mother, father, brothers, sisters, grandparents etc.

(2) How many children have babies in their family?

(3) Remind children that babies come in different sizes:
   some have long legs, some with hair,
   some without hair, some big, some small.

(4) Talk about how fast babies change and grow.

ACTIVITIES

- Draw your family. If time permits show each family picture to each other.
- Draw you as a baby in your family.
- Turn to the child next to you and name the thing you can do now that you couldn't do as a baby (babies have special needs).
- Find out what age you learned to crawl, take first steps, speak first words etc.

PAUSE and REFLECT

Music – assemble quietly on the carpet.

Place candle safely in centre and arrange family pictures around it and pray for families.

PRAYER

Loving Father,
thank you for my mum, dad, brothers, sisters
and all who love and care for me.
Amen.

LEARNING OBJECTIVE

Children know and understand that they are growing and developing as members of their own family and God's family.

KEYWORDS
Unique
Friend
God
Important
Different
Special

SKILLS
Listening
Observing
Relating
Speaking
Respecting
Praying
Reflecting
Understanding

YEAR ONE

A Journey in Love

1

SOCIAL

BACKGROUND NOTES

The reason children were asked to find out what age first steps/first words occurred was to draw out the social dimension of human growth and development within the family and the development of social skills.

(1) Invite children to share their home research.

(2) Parents share the wonder and excitement of these moments of growth and development for them.

ACTIVITIES

- How do we help and care for others at home e.g. Help with baby, tidy room, lay the table, wash up?
- Talk about safe and realistic ways of helping at home.
- Write on card each identified quality and give each child a card.

PAUSE and REFLECT

Music – assemble quietly and think about all the wonderful things we have heard about the wonder and beauty of our first steps, words etc.

In the quiet of our hearts we share in our families.

PRAYER

*Thank you Lord,
for all who love and care for us.*

Amen.

EMOTIONAL

(1) What are the happiest moments in your family?
  e.g. birthdays, christenings, weddings.

(2) What are the saddest moments in your family?
  e.g. death of pets, leaving home.

(3) How is love shown in your family?

A Journey in Love YEAR ONE | 17

ACTIVITIES

- Divide children into four groups to create:
    a) two happy experiences of family and
    b) two sad experiences of family.
- Share each role play with class.
- Talk about the ideas expressed in each role play.

PAUSE and REFLECT

Stand and form a circle, hold hands and sing:
'WE ARE THE CHURCH'
CHRISTOPHER WALKER

PRAYER

Thank you, Lord,
for all the happy moments we share in our families.

Amen.

INTELLECTUAL

BACKGROUND NOTES

The family is the children's first experience of love and loving relationships.

(1) Why do we need to grow up in families?

(2) What happens if you grow up without a family? Would it be a happy experience?

(3) What would you miss? How would life be different?

ACTIVITIES

- Read or show a relevant clip from *Jungle Book* by Rudyad Kipling ...the need for family as exemplified in this story.
- Need for family – who takes the place of mum and dad for Mowgli?
- What other family do you belong to besides your personal family.
- Bring in reminders of Baptism e.g. candle, photograph.

PAUSE and REFLECT

Reflective music.

PRAYER

Loving Father,
we thank you that we are growing and developing as members of our own family and your family –
and so we pray our family prayer: Our Father...

YEAR ONE

1

SPIRITUAL

BACKGROUND NOTES

It is assumed that children will have covered Baptism in 'Here I Am'.

(1) We are members of God's family.

(2) How were we born into God's family?

(3) What special title do we give to God as members of God's family?
e.g. Our Father, Jesus our Brother,
Holy Spirit our Friend and Guide.

PLENARY

Music, artefact / pictures of Holy Family, own familes, class family, candle.

Give thanks for all our families.

PRAYER

Sign of the Cross using the following:

From my head to my heart,
from my shoulder to my shoulder,
I believe in you my God,
my Father.
Amen.

A Journey in Love

YEAR TWO

We meet God's love in the community

PHYSICAL

(1) Do you belong to a community?
(2) What other community do you belong to?
(3) How do you belong to these communities?

BACKGROUND NOTES

Definition of the word Community
1. The people living in one locality.
2. A group of people having cultural or other characteristics in common.

Collins Dictionary

ACTIVITIES

- Look at the word community...
  Develop with children an awareness that belonging to their family is their first experience of a community of love.
  Encourage children to share:
  - How love is shown in the family.
  - What activities are done together.
  - How they look out for each other.
  - Inside a heart frame draw a family activity they enjoy.

- Focus on the School as Community, e.g. Class community, Year Community, School Community, Parish Community, Club Communities (in and out of school).

- Discuss signs of belonging, e.g. uniform, attendance, commitment, loyalty.
  - respect for the well-being of others
  - contribution to team spirit
  - celebrating each others gifts/abilities and achievements.

LEARNING OBJECTIVE

Children know and understand that they are growing and developing in a God-given community.

KEYWORDS

God
Community
Belonging
Family
Father/Mother
Carer/Guardian
Feelings
Emotions

SKILLS

Listening
Observing
Relating
Speaking
Respecting
Reflecting
Praying
Understanding

YEAR TWO

A Journey in Love

2

PAUSE and REFLECT

Gather in a circle and celebrate the gift of living in different communities.

PRAYER

Taizé music – Invite each child to give thanks for a particular community, e.g. thank you for my family...

SOCIAL

(1) Is belonging to a community important?

(2) What do we receive from the community we belong to?

(3) What do we give to the community we belong to?

ACTIVITIES

- Invite into the school key community members, e.g. priest, doctor, community police-officer, caretaker, refuse collector, dentist, florist, nurse...
- Reflect with children on the different services to the community of invited guests (as listed above).
- Invite children to share their contribution to their communities to which they belong.
  How can they make a difference?
- Write in cloud shapes 'DREAMS', 'ASPIRATIONS', 'PROMISES'.

PAUSE and REFLECT

Gather together – reflective music.

Share aspirations, dreams and promises.

Sing: 'O LORD, ALL THE WORLD BELONGS TO YOU.'

Celebration Hymnal for Everyone no.567

PRAYER

*Bless our communities
and make us all more helpful.*

Amen.

A Journey in Love   YEAR TWO | 21

EMOTIONAL

(1) How does a community help us to develop our feelings and emotions?

(2) Are we always happy in our community?

(3) Are we, as a community, sometimes sad or upset?

ACTIVITIES

- Divide into groups – Role Play different scenarios in the communities to which you belong,
    e.g. a happy event, a sad event, a jealous or hurtful experience.

PAUSE and REFLECT

Gather together – reflective music.

Think about the amazing love of God for each one.

Remember: He is with us at all times.

PRAYER

*Loving Father,
we thank you for your love
   and closeness to us always,
particularly in our communities.
Amen.*

INTELLECTUAL

(1) Could people feel alone even though they belong to a community?

(2) What would they miss out on?

(3) What are the advantages of being on your own?

YEAR TWO

A Journey in Love

2

ACTIVITIES

- Are there lonely children in this school? How do you recognise that children have no friends? How can we help?
- Discuss the disadvantages of being on your own.
- Consider the advantages of being on your own, e.g. time for homework, time to think, time to pray, time to read and write.

PAUSE and REFLECT

Gather together.

Listen to Jesus speak these words to you: *"I am with you always."*

Share a gesture of friendship:

Sign of Peace and Love.

PRAYER

The peace of the Lord be always with us.

Amen.

SPIRITUAL

(1) If God is called 'Our Father' what does that make us?

(2) As children of God how should we treat each other?

Sing: BIND US TOGETHER or WHEN I NEEDED A NEIGHBOUR.

PLENARY

We celebrate that we are all brothers and sisters in the God-filled community of home and school as we hold hands and pray the Family Prayer

PRAYER

Our Father...

YEAR THREE

How we live in love

PHYSICAL

(1) Who takes care of me?

(2) How do I look after myself?
e.g, safety, crossing the road, healthy eating.

(3) How am I changing?

ACTIVITIES

- List/discuss the various people who care for you at home, at school, in the Parish and in the community.

  Home research: collect/design and draw pictures/photographs to illustrate above.

  Share the different categories and aspects of caring by all those identified above.

- Focus on ways of growing healthily and keeping safe, e.g. eating healthily, regular exercise, (see science topic teeth and eating) rules of the road, school rules, positive relationships, community involvement.

- Look at photographs of yourselves taken over the years and note the changes in your growth and development.

LEARNING OBJECTIVES

Children know and understand the virtues essential to friendship, e.g. loyalty, responsibility... and experience the importance both of forgiving and being forgiven and of celebrating God's forgiveness.

SKILLS

*Listening
Observing
Relating
Speaking
Respecting
Reflecting
Praying
Understanding*

YEAR THREE

A Journey in Love

3

PAUSE and REFLECT

Think about all the people we have talked about in this lesson.
All those whose photgraphs are displayed.

PRAYER

Generous God,

bless and care for them.

Amen.

SOCIAL

(1) How do I keep myself safe?

(2) How do I help others to make and keep friends?

(3) How do I take care of others?

ACTIVITIES

- Discuss and expand on ways children can take care of their families and friends,

    e.g. in school: looking out for new children, friendship stop, read poem 'The Loner' by Julie Holder,

    e.g. at home: Younger brothers and sisters, cousins, role in the family.

- Look at ways of making and keeping a friend,

    e.g. always being there for others, class friendships, circle time, playground games and friendships.

- Become more aware of others and their needs,

    e.g. new children to the class and school, children sick or going through trauma. Being quick to forgive and forget upsets.

THE LONER

He leans against the playground wall,
Smacks his hands against the bricks
And other boredom-beating tricks,
Traces patterns with his feet,
Scuffs to make the tarmac squeak,
Back against the wall he stays
And never plays.

The playground's quick with life,
The beat is strong. Though sharp as a knife
Strife doesn't last long.
There is shouting, laughter, song,
And a place at the wall
For who won't belong.

We pass him running, skipping, walking,
In slow huddled groups, low talking.
Each in our familiar clique
We pass him by and never speak,
His loneness is his shell and shield
And neither he nor we will yield.

He wasn't there at the wall today,
Someone said he'd moved away
To another school and place
And on the wall where he used to lean

Someone had chalked
'Watch this space.'

Julie Holder

A Journey in Love — YEAR THREE | 25

> **PAUSE and REFLECT**
> We raise up to the Lord all those we have mentioned in this lesson.
>
> **PRAYER**
> *Bless our friends and help me to be a better friend.*
> *Amen.*

EMOTIONAL

(1) How do you feel when a friend is not there for you?

(2) How do your friends feel when you are not there for them?

(3) How can you be a more supportive friend?

> **ACTIVITIES**
> - Read a story highlighting how a friend feels when they are not helped,
>   *e.g. 'Dogger'* by Shirly Hughes.
>   Reflect on how it feels to be let down by a friend.
> - How does your friend feel when let down by you.
>   Share what we mean by a supportive friend: loyalty, trust, listening, understanding, forgiving, reliability.
> - Compose a friendship promise of supportiveness.
>   Illustrate and share with your friend.
>   Introduce: Friend of the Day, Friend of the Week.

> **PAUSE and REFLECT**
> Children share their friendship promises.
>
> **PRAYER**
> *Forgive us, Lord, for the times we have not been a true friend.*
> *Amen.*

YEAR THREE — 3

A Journey in Love

INTELLECTUAL

(1) Can you recognise the difference between being alone and being lonely?

(2) To recognise the need for personal privacy, e.g. personal space.

ACTIVITIES

- Discuss the difference between being alone and being lonely. Use relevant photographs/press cuttings/poems and music to illustrate how some people are alone and happy and others although surrounded by people are very lonely.
  Explore together reasons why this can be.

- Consider the meaning of 'personal space'.
  Reflect on its importance in our lives to: calm ourselves down when we get angry, think and see a better way of acting and behaving, praying, researching and so on.

PAUSE and REFLECT

Gather in a friendship circle and encourage children to sit beside someone they seldom choose to be with.

Share a sign of peace and friendship.

PRAYER

Thank you God for _____ (name the person beside me) and bless our time together in school. Amen.

A Journey in Love

SPIRITUAL

(1) Read or sing the story of Zacchaeus who was an outcast. Jesus accepted him as a friend, welcomed and forgave him.

(2) How can I forgive and include others as Jesus did?

(3) Write on a card what you like about your friend and share. Take the card home and keep in a special place.

> **PAUSE and REFLECT**
>
> Sign of peace and friendship.
>
> **PRAYER**
>
> Pray together (in song with actions if preferred) the 'Our Father'.

YEAR FOUR

God loves us in our differences

PHYSICAL

LEARNING OBJECTIVES

Children know and understand that they are all different and celebrate these differences as they appreciate that God's love accepts us as we are and as we change.

(1) Continue to recognise that all pupils grow and develop at a different rate.

(2) Name the different male and female body parts and introduce their various functions.

(3) Identify the development of the baby in the womb.

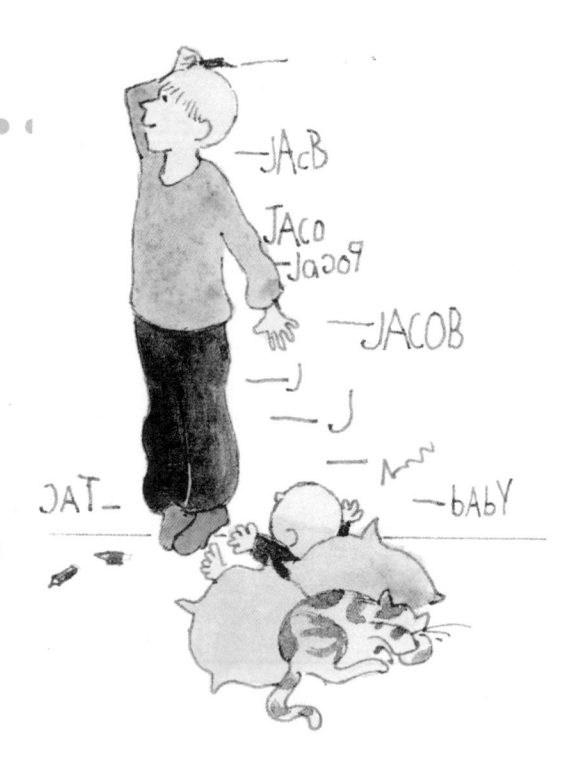

KEYWORDS

God / Gifts
Talents
Difference
Developement
Change
Male and female body parts
Conflict
Appreciate
Celebrate
Achievement

SKILLS

Sensitivity
Respect

ACTIVITIES

- Notice the physical differences in class e.g. not all children are the same height.
  Observe the height differences in other year groups.
  Notice that each member of staff is unique and different and accepts themselves and others as they are.

- Select school resources which highlight and illustrate the different male and female parts of the body and introduce their various functions.

- Use the images on the following page and any other school resources to illustrate the development of the baby in the womb.

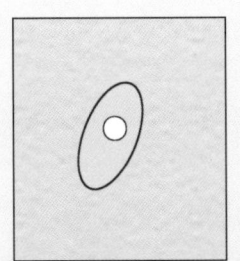

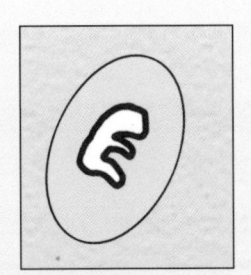

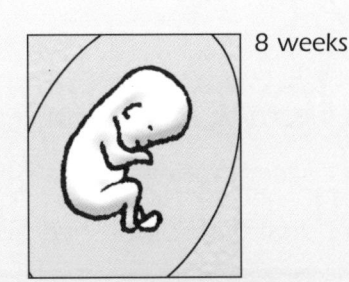

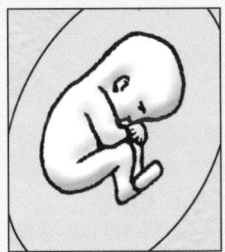

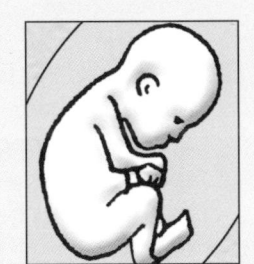

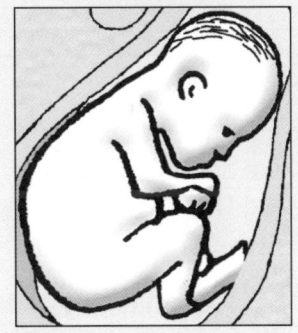

A Journey in Love

YEAR FOUR

Conception
4 weeks
8 weeks
12 weeks
16 weeks
20 weeks

The baby grows in the womb

Conception	The baby is just large enough to see. He/she is about half the size of a full stop.
4 weeks	His/her heart is formed and he/she has small leg and arm buds.
8 weeks	The baby's eyes and ears are developing and legs show knees and ankles; toes are joined together.
12 weeks	All the important parts are formed and nails begin to grow.
16 weeks	Some bones are hardening. The mother can feel movements and the baby can suck his/her thumb.
20 weeks	The baby is now 25-27cm long. His/her fingernails and toenails are fully grown.

PAUSE and REFLECT

Consider how God has made me. Consider the wonder of me as I grow and develope.

PRAYER

For the wonder of me,
  Thank you Lord.
For the uniqueness of all of us,
  We thank you Lord.
For the wonder of your love in creating us.
  We thank you Lord. Amen

SOCIAL

(1) How do I learn to accept and celebrate who I am?

(2) How do I accept difference in others?

(3) How do I deal with difference and manage the conflicts that arise?

ACTIVITIES

- Ask children to think of three things they like about themselves and three things they are good at.
  Name one thing they dislike in themselves and one thing they are not good at.
  Encourage children to think about their personal qualities as well as their skills and talents.
  Devise a character sketch of their talents, skills, likes and dislikes.

- Distribute a small piece of paper to every child with the name of their class friend on it. Ask the children to think carefully about that person and write one thing that that person is really good at. Collect papers and share the responses with class.

- Discuss with class:
  Do we all have the same talents? Are we all good at the same things? What would our world be like if we all had the same talents?

- Sit in a circle with the children and ask: What is conflict?
  Ask the children to talk to the person next to them and share their ideas.
  Ask the children to share a definition of the word 'conflict' and share with the whole class. What conflict do we have at home, school, in the playground and in clubs?

PAUSE and REFLECT

For the times we have been in conflict with others at home, at school and in our community.

Forgive us, Lord.

Amen.

A Journey in Love   YEAR FOUR | 31

EMOTIONAL

(1) How do I appreciate my own gifts, talents, achievements and all that makes me unique?

(2) How do I appreciate others and the gifts they have been given?

(3) How do I deal with the natural, negative emotions that present themselves?

ACTIVITIES

- List your gifts, talents and achievements.
- Share list with partner and invite partner to add to the list.
- Name and identify the natural negative emotions,
  e.g. anger, envy, gluttony, jealousy, spitefulness.
- Is there someone you can talk to about these emotions?

PAUSE and REFLECT

In silence think about our discussions and the gifts and talents we all have.

We praise and thank God now.

PRAYER

For your gifts, talents and many blessings to us.

We thank you, Lord.

Amen.

INTELLECTUAL

(1) Can I identify and name my feelings?

(2) Do I know and understand what these feelings are?

(3) How do I deal with what I feel, and can I analyse my feelings and actions?

ACTIVITIES

- Categorise happy and sad feelings.
- Why am I a mixture of happy and sad feelings – Is everyone like this?

YEAR FOUR — A Journey in Love

4

> **PAUSE and REFLECT**
>
> Reflect on what we have recognised as our positive and happy feelings.
>
> **PRAYER**
>
> *Lord, you are always with us,*
> *in happy and sad times.*
> *For your constant love,*
> **We thank you.**
>
> *Amen.*

SPIRITUAL

(1) St Paul's teaching on love....

> Love is patient and kind; it is not jealous or conceited or proud;
> love is not ill-mannered or selfish or irritable;
> love does not keep a record of wrongs;
> love is not happy with evil, but is happy with the truth.
> Love never gives up; and its faith, hope, and patience never fail.

1 Corinthians 13:4–7

(2) Sing: 'PEACE, PERFECT PEACE...'

Celebration Hymnal for Everyone no.597
(Verse 2 only)

> **PAUSE and REFLECT**
>
> Select a phrase:
>
> Am I always patient...
>
> Am I always kind...
>
> Am I always loving...
>
> **PRAYER**
>
> *O Lord,*
> *it was you who created my being*
> *and knit me together in my*
>   *mother's womb.*
>
> *I praise and thank you for*
> *the wonder of my being,*
> *for all my gifts and talents.*
>
> *I praise and thank you for*
> *the gifts and talents of all in my*
>   *class and school.*
>
> *Amen.*

YEAR FIVE

God loves me in my changing and development

PHYSICAL and INTELLECTUAL

(1) Identify and celebrate the ways I have changed since birth.

(2) Discuss the external and internal changes which happen to boys and girls in puberty.

Physical changes in Girls
- breasts develop: they come in all shapes and sizes
- hips broaden and waist slims
- ovaries produce oestrogen
- hormonal activity
- menstruation begins
- uterus enlarges
- vaginal lining thickens
- first menstruation approximately 12 months after breasts have begun to develop
- usually start to grow hair on underarm, pubic area and legs

Physical changes in Boys
- testosterone for boys carried in the blood stream and triggers changes
- muscles and bones develop
- voice deepens
- some boys get uneven breast changes in early puberty
- waist thickens
- longer limbs in proportion to body
- shoulders broaden
- wet dreams and erections
- penis and scrotum enlarge
- hair can grow on face, chest, back, arms as well as under arms and pubic area
- production of sperm and discharge of seminal fluid during ejaculation
- adam's apple enlarges

RELATIONSHIPS IN MORAL EDUCATION (draft document), Catholic Education Commission, Scotland 2000

LEARNING OBJECTIVES

Children know and become aware of the physical and emotional changes that accompany puberty - sensitivity, mood swings, anger, boredom, etc. and grow further in their understanding of God's presence in their daily lives.

KEYWORDS
God
Sensitivity
Puberty
Presence
Celebrate
External
Internal
Change
Develop
Ovulation

YEAR FIVE

A Journey in Love

(3) Recognise that sexual development is a natural part of human growth and that physical changes from child to adult means the ability and potential to become a mother or father.

The purposes of the menstrual cycle is to prepare the female body for reproduction.

There are two important stages:

KEYWORDS
Reproduction
Ovulation
Production
Hormones
Menstruation

SKILLS
Categorising
Observing
Classifying
Listening
Questioning
Speaking
Relating
Respecting
Reflecting
Thinking
Identifying
Accepting
Empathising
Understanding
Communicating
Presenting
Evaluating
Researching

1. Menstruation
(From the Latin for 'month')

The menstrual cycle is controlled by hormones released from the pituitary gland. Most menstrual cycles last for about 28 days. The first day of the period marks the start of the cycle and is counted as day 1.

If the uterus does not receive a fertilised ovum, the lining of the uterus breaks down and is shed over the next number of days. This is called menstruation.

The lining of the uterus begins to thicken and an ovum begins to develop.

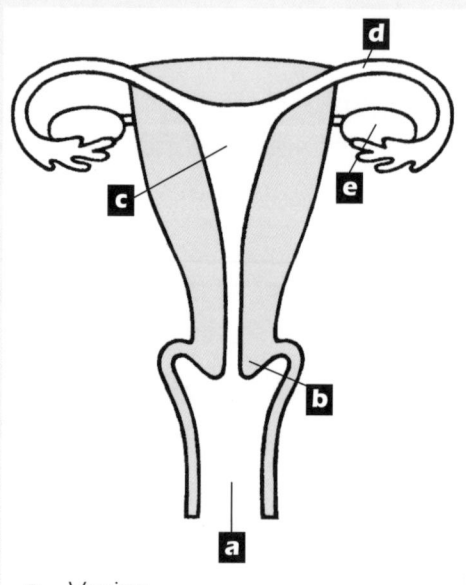

a. Vagina
b. Cervix
c. Womb (Uterus)
d. Fallopian tube
e. Ovary

2. Ovulation

On approximately the 14th day of the cycle an ovum is released into the fallopian tube. This is called ovulation.

The ovum travels towards the uterus.

The lining of the uterus continues to thicken and gets full of blood in case a fertilised ovum arrives.

If the ovum is not fertilised it will dissolve and a period will occur. Then the cycle starts again.

A Journey in Love

> **PAUSE and REFLECT**
> Think about and celebrate how I am growing and developing.
>
> **PRAYER**
> *Giver and Protector of life,*
> *guide me as I grow and develop.*
> *Amen.*

SOCIAL/EMOTIONAL

(1) Recognise behaviour changes as we grow up. Expectations are different and are often dependent on our experiences, and treatment by others, and our view of the world in which we live.

(2) Reflect on ways to become more sensitive to the emotional development of oneself and others.

Social and emotional changes

- easily embarrassed
- need for privacy
- moods swings up and down without much warning
- divided loyalty may occur between self, friends and parents
- production of hormones triggers sexual desire, arousal and urge
- evolving a set of values and moral codes
- seeking independence
- risk-taking behaviour
- concern for the future
- identity formation

RELATIONSHIPS IN MORAL EDUCATION
(draft document),
Catholic Education Commission,
Scotland 2000

> **PAUSE and REFLECT**
> In silence reflect on all that we have discussed and thank God for his gifts.
>
> **PRAYER**
> *Loving Lord,*
> *Help us to respect and understand each other better*
> *as we continue to change and grow.*
> *Amen.*

SPIRITUAL

GATHERING MUSIC

> To live is to change
> and to be perfect
> is to have changed often.
>
> Cardinal Newman

(1) Ask children to share their understanding of change through poetry, prayer, art etc.

(2) Share with each other and celebrate the wonder of change.

CONCLUDING PRAYER
(SERENITY PRAYER)

*God, grant me the serenity
to accept the things I cannot change;
Courage to change the things I can,
and the wisdom to know the difference.*

Amen.

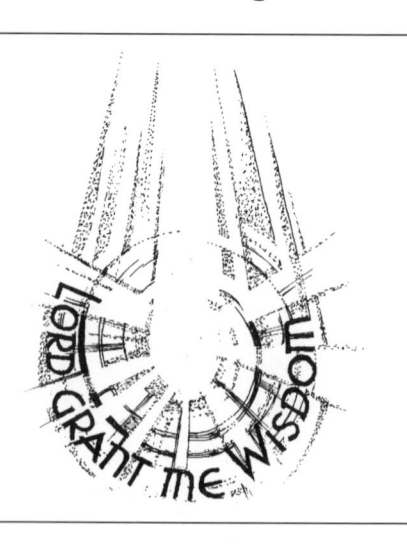

A Friendship Blessing

May you be blessed with good friends.

May you learn to be a good friend to yourself.

May you be able to journey to that place in your soul
where there is great love, warmth, feeling and forgiveness.

May this change you.

John O'Donohue

YEAR SIX

The wonder of God's love in creating new life

BACKGROUND NOTE

The Christian teaching is that babies should be conceived as the fruit of a loving, married relationship.

The Circle of Life and Love

Every human being is caught up in the circle of life and love.

1 The circle is one of love's development and expression. A couple 'make love' (their sexual union is, ideally, an expression of love); if a child is conceived, it needs love from its first recognised moments. It is surrounded by love as it grows and develops.
As it matures away from a self-centred love, the child/young person learns how to give love and not just receive it. In maturity the woman/man looks instinctively for a marriage partner with whom the loving gift of self can find expression in love's deepest sign: sexual intercourse, they make love.

LOVE CIRCLE: Marriage → 'Make love' → New Life → Self-centred → Give and take of love → First signs of romantic love → Choosing a fiancé(e) → Marriage

LEARNING OBJECTIVES

Children develop, in an appropriate way for their age, an understanding of sexuality and grow further in their appreciation of their dignity and worth as children of God.

KEYWORDS
God
Christian
Appropriate
Dignity
Sexuality
Intercourse
Fallopian
Conceive
Relationship
Uterus
Cervix
Marriage
Fiancé
Fiancée

YEAR SIX

A Journey in Love

6

SKILLS
Categorising
Observing
Classifying
Listening
Questioning
Speaking
Relating
Respecting
Reflecting
Thinking
Identifying
Accepting
Empathising
Understanding
Communicating
Presenting
Evaluating
Researching

2 Love proclaims its presence by signs and the deepest, most intimate and most wonderful of human signs of love is the gift of self in sexual intercourse. But the natural outcome (all conditions being fulfilled) of sexual intercourse is the conception of new life. As co-creators the parents bestow life on a new human being. That human being needs love and will, in time, express love: will make love, and a new human being will join us! To remove 'life', 'love' or 'sex' from the circle destroys God's intended balance and produces severe problems for society.

Love is indeed 'ecstacy' not in the sense of a moment of intoxication.

Deus Caritas Est 6

> We are not some casual and meaningless product of evolution. Each of us is the result of a thought of God.
>
> Benedict XVI

A Journey in Love   YEAR SIX | 39

PHYSICAL

(1) Explain how human life is conceived.

Look at the illustrations of the organs of the human body including male and female reproductive organs.

Anatomy

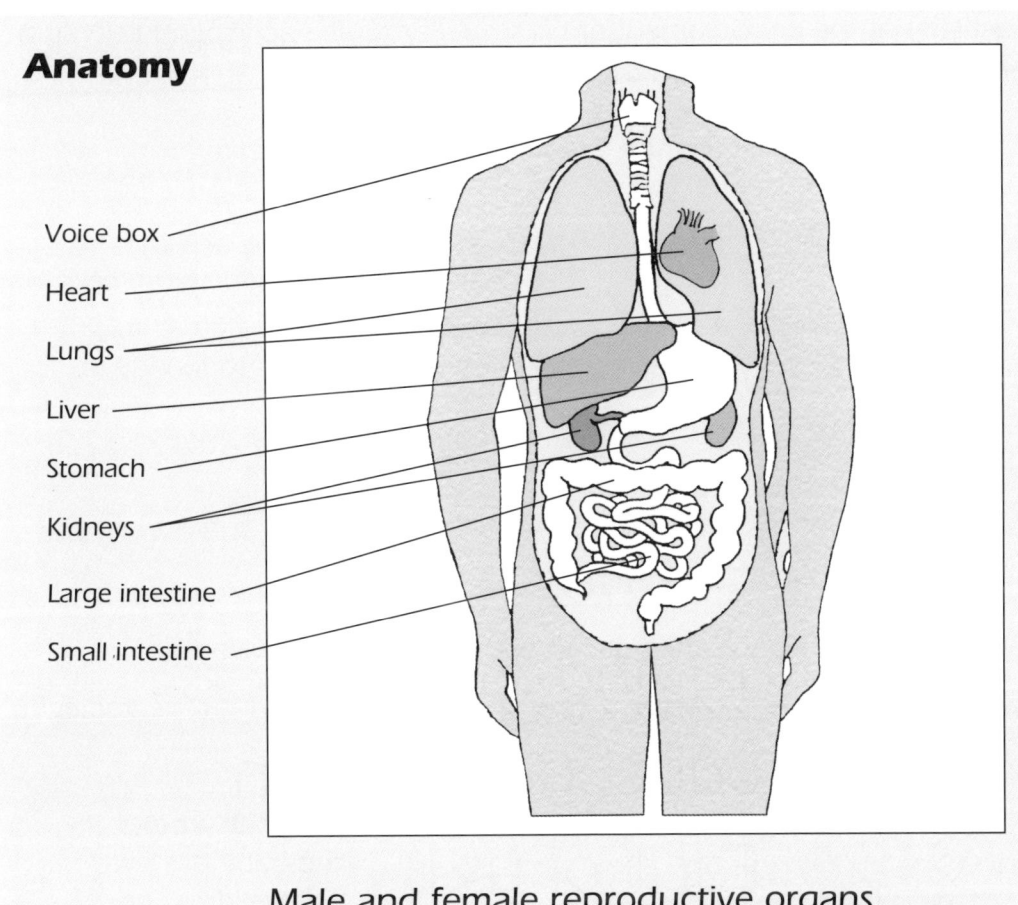

Voice box
Heart
Lungs
Liver
Stomach
Kidneys
Large intestine
Small intestine

Male and female reproductive organs

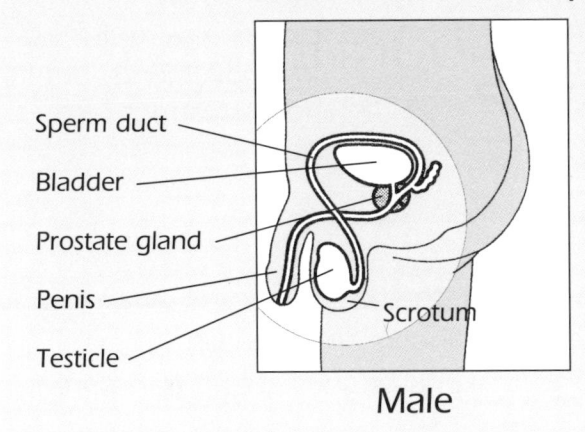

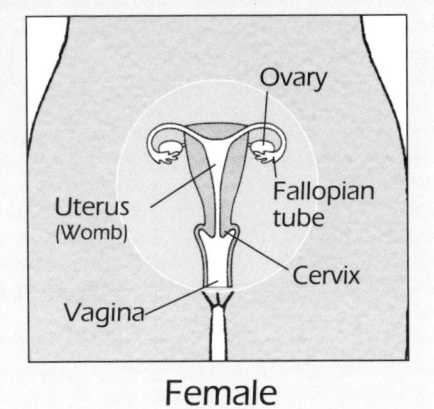

Sperm duct
Bladder
Prostate gland
Penis
Testicle
Scrotum

Male

Ovary
Uterus (Womb)
Fallopian tube
Cervix
Vagina

Female

YEAR SIX

A Journey in Love

6

Sexual intercourse between husband and wife is a joyful expression of their love for each other.
It is an act of self-giving, made by two people who want to give everything of themselves to the person they love and respect.

When a couple make love the husband's penis becomes stiff and is placed inside his wife's vagina. Millions of sperm cells are released when the man ejaculates at the peak moment of his sexual arousal. Each sperm cell has a long tail that it uses to swim through the cervix, into the uterus, and eventually into the wife's fallopian tubes.

Relationships in Moral Education p.23

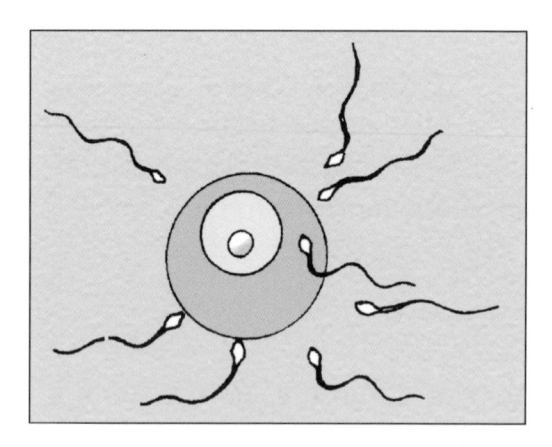

Although a hundred sperm cells may reach the egg cell only one sperm can enter the egg to fertilise it.

(2) Understand how a child grows within the mother's womb.

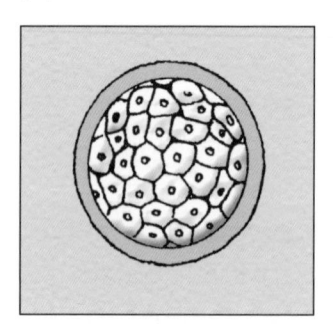

After a few days, the cell divides repeatedley to form a ball of cells.

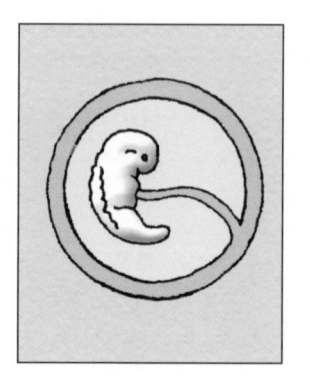

After 8 weeks, the baby has eyes but no eyelids.

It starts making its first tiny movements, but its mother cannot feel them yet.

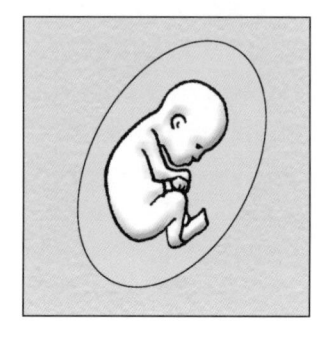

After 16 weeks, the baby begins to swallow and pass urine. It has fingers and toenails.
At this stage its skin is bright red and transparent.

A Journey in Love

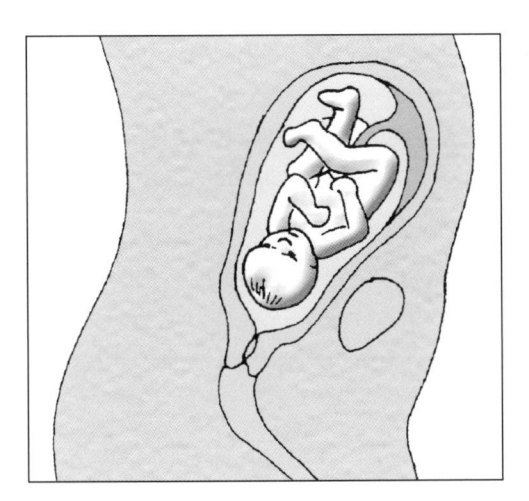

YEAR SIX | 41

After 24 weeks, the baby can hear voices and other sounds from outside its mother.
It has some hair and eyebrows and eyelashes. Its skin is very wrinkled.

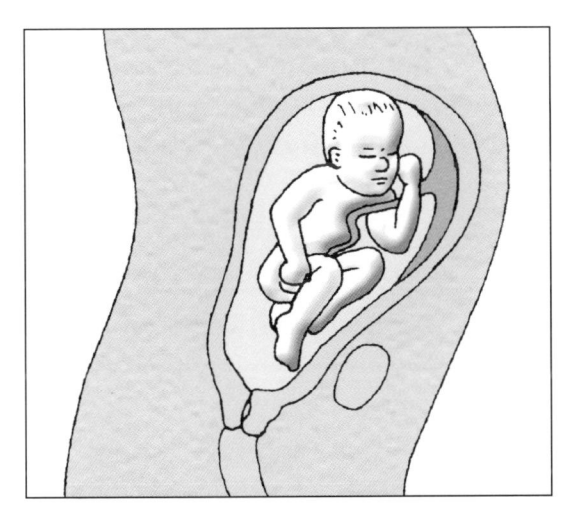

After 28 weeks, the baby's kicks are quite strong and can be felt by putting a hand on the mother's tummy.

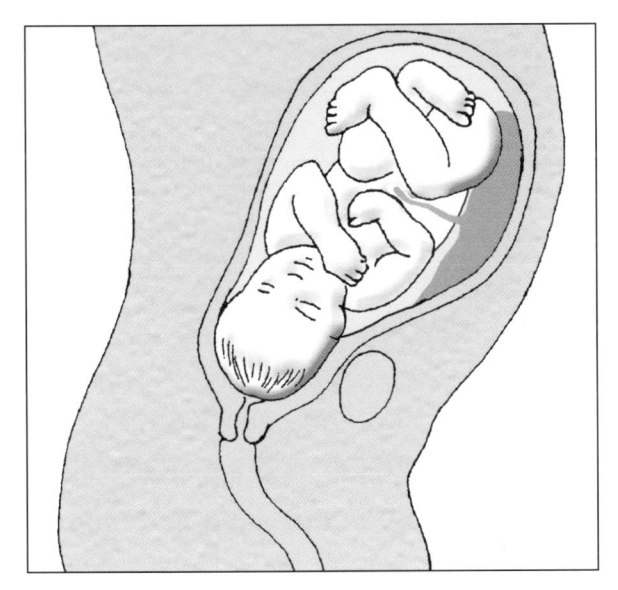

After 36 weeks, the baby has taken up its final position in the uterus. Its lungs are getting ready to take their first breath. The baby continues to get fatter. Some time after 36 weeks, the baby's head is now positioned ready for birth. The baby could arrive any time between 38th and 42nd week of pregnancy.

YEAR SIX

A Journey in Love

> **PAUSE and REFLECT**
>
> *For the beauty and gift of love,*
> *We thank you Lord.*
>
> *For mothers and fathers,*
> *We thank you Lord.*
>
> *For doctors and nurses,*
> *We thank you Lord.*
>
> *For all babies and the miracle of new life,*
> *We thank you Lord.*
>
> *Amen.*

EMOTIONAL

Relationships develop and eventually, you may be able to use the word love.

This has to be explained: real love reveals itself in complete commitment. Often we use the word love too casually, the claim to love someone is a momentous one.

If one is in love with another, certain characteristics follow:

1. Love is caring and sharing with another person. We can love many people. However, two people can be drawn to a love that at its deeper levels become more and more exclusive. Intimacies are shared with the loved one and not with others.

2. There is need for a basis for love, which is not only one-dimensional, such as, a common interest in music, sexual attraction, a shared interest in sport. A basis for love needs to grow and develop, so that, the two people are more and more generous in their shared love.

3. The relationship requires time to mature and develop and ultimately people may decide to get married.

A Journey in Love

4. Without love, relationships will fail because living with another human being means that they will find out exactly what you are like, what kind of person you are (knowledge).

5. It comes back to the kind of person you are, and what qualities you bring to that relationship.

PAUSE and REFLECT

Consider ways that enable happy relationships.

Consider ways that relationships can be unhappy.

PRAYER

Source of Love, help us to love and respect each other
and enjoy the beauty of
*   happy friendships.*
Amen.

SOCIAL

(1) Recognise and compile a list of the signs of love expressed in those around us,
    e.g. signs of love between those who care for us, loving couples, older people.

(2) Reflect on the different degrees of friendship that exist,
    e.g. school friends, close friends, best friends, mixed gender friends, life-long friends.

PRAYER

Jesus, our friend and brother, embrace in your love all our friends.
Amen.

YEAR SIX

A Journey in Love

SPIRITUAL

(1) Understand that God causes new life to begin through the love that parents have for each other.

(2) Celebrate God's creative love in creating us as his children and recognise that we grow as human beings to the extent we give and receive love. The on-going understanding of marriage is living out love.

(3) As Christians we can appreciate the sheer wonder of the sexual act. God created the incredible natural process by which husband and wife bring new life into the world. The Church celebrates all this in the Sacrament of Marriage.

> "Marriage based on exclusive and definitive love becomes the icon of the relationship between God and his people and visa versa. God's way of loving becomes the measure of human love."
>
> Deus Caritas Est 11

A Journey in Love

YEAR SIX | 45

Celebration of friendship and life

GATHERING MUSIC

(1) Introduction

We have been thinking and celebrating the joy, wonder and beauty of our journey of love which began when we were conceived, born and supported to this moment.

OPENING PRAYER

> Generous God,
> We give thanks for the gift of life;
> for our mums and dads and
> for the gift of being a child of God.
>
> Amen.

(2) Sing… 'MY GOD LOVES ME'.   Celebration Hymnal for Everyone no.499

(3) A large candle is lighted reminding us of God's love which called us into being and embraces us at all moments of our lives.

(4) Symbols of our Baptism and our families are placed around the candle.

(5) Samples of our study of God's creative love in this programme are brought forward also.

(6) Reading (JEREMIAH 1:5)

> I chose you before I gave you life and before you were born selected you to be a prophet to the nations.

(7) Individual candles are lit from the large candle and children renew their baptismal promises.

(8) **PRAYER**

*We praise and thank you, Lord,
for gifts of life and love.*

*Help us to use these wisely
as we to continue to journey in love.*

Amen.

(9) Conclude with hymn/song…

'LET THERE BE LOVE SHARED AMONG US'.

Celebration Hymnal no.358

Journey of Life

For each of us, life is like a journey.

Birth is the beginning of this journey,

And death is not the end; but the destination.

It is a journey that takes us
From youth to age,
From innocence to awareness,
From ignorance to knowledge,
From foolishness to wisdom,
From weakness to strength and often back again,
From offence to forgiveness,
From pain to compassion,
From fear to faith,
From defeat to victory and from victory to defeat,
Until, looking backward or ahead,
We see that victory does not lie

At some high point along the way,

But in having made the journey,

Stage by stage.

Adapted from an old Hebrew prayer.

Some perspectives on marriage

Scriptural foundation

THE IDEAL PLACE to be informed about any of the sacraments is the General Instruction issued on each of them after Vatican II. Therefore we need to grasp the key ideas about marriage from its instruction, supplemented by the section on marriage in the Catechism of the Catholic Church (1602–1658.) An account of an ecclesial view of marriage can be found in Ecclesia: A Theological Encyclopedia of the Church, pub. Liturgical Press, pp 285-289. Marriage as a human institution is found in all cultures. It was regarded as God-centred in the Old Testament, particularly in Genesis:

> He created them male and female, blessed them, and said, "Have many children, so that your many descendants will live all over the earth and bring it under control. I am putting you in charge of the fish, the birds and all the wild animals." (Gen. 1:28) That is why a man leaves his father and mother and is united with his wife and they become one (Gen. 2:24).

The marriage relationship of husband and wife became an image of God's covenant relationship with God's people.

> Your Creator will be like a husband to you – the Lord Almighty is his name. The holy God of Israel will save you, he is the ruler of all the world. Israel, you are like a young wife deserted by her husband and deeply distressed. But the Lord calls you back to him and says: "For one brief moment I left you; with deep love I will take you back, I turned away angry for only a moment, but I will show you my love forever." So says the Lord who saves you. (Isaiah 54:5-8)

This covenant relationship was often broken by the people though the love of God, the spouse remains faithful.

> The Lord told me to proclaim this message to everyone in Jerusalem. Remember how faithful you were when you were young, how you loved me when we were first married; you followed me through the desert, through a land that had not been sown. (Jer. 2:2)

Jesus re-established the original intentions of God with regard to marriage:

> Jesus answered, "Haven't you read the scripture that says that in the beginning the Creator made people male and female? And God said, 'For this reason a man will leave his father and mother and unite with his wife, and the two will become one.' So they are no longer two, but one. Man must not separate, then, what God has joined together."
>
> The Pharisees asked him, "Why, then, did Moses give the law for a man to hand his wife a divorce notice and send her away?" Jesus answered, "Moses gave you permission to divorce your wives because you are so hard to teach. But it was not like that at the time of creation. I tell you, then, that any man who divorces his wife for any cause other than her unfaithfulness, commits adultery if he marries some other woman."

Matt. 19:4-9

Marriage, love and family were highly regarded by the New Testament. Throughout its history, the Church has always shared its concern for marriage, a concern expressed in legislation and teaching.

> The Catechism states: On the threshold of his public life Jesus performs his first sign – at his mother's request – during a wedding feast. The Church attaches great importance to Jesus' presence at the wedding at Cana. She sees in it the confirmation of the goodness of marriage and the proclamation that thenceforth marriage will be an efficacious sign of Christ's presence. CCC [n.1613]

Four moments

In his article on marriage in, The New Dictionary of Catholic Spirituality Liturgical Press 1993, David H Thomas expressed the view that the spirituality of marriage can be divided into four moments or phases which can be seen as having both a chronological and developmental dimension. But like the seasons of the year, these phases can be appreciated as each coming in its own time without any priority of importance being assumed: solitude, commitment, generativity and marriage and the Eucharist.

Solitude, he asserts recognises that every Christian stands before God and all other persons as a free, differentiated person who possesses: a unique personality, distinctive ideas and feelings and a purpose for being unlike any other created being. In marriage, both persons should retain their individuality as well as their duality.

Secondly, the heart of marriage is the mutual commitment of both persons (man and woman) to share life for better or for worse: sharing one's time and energy, love shared physically, emotionally, sexually and spiritually.

The third phase is generativity. In all cultures the ideal situation for children to enter the world is in a stable family. The view of marriage in the past was, however, too narrowly focussed on generation. But it still retains an essential place in Christian marriage even though we now see other dimensions of the sacrament.

Finally, marriage like all elements of the Christian life finds its highest expression in the Eucharist, "the source and summit of the Christian life" (Vatican II, Church LG11. From the Word celebrated at Mass and from the sacrament received, parents, and later their children, receive guidance and strength. All problems can be brought to the Eucharist for healing and wisdom.

Mission

The other aspect of the Church's life is 'mission' which points to the service of others. Clothing the naked, visiting the sick... Taking this a stage further Christian marriage contains its own communion (the love between the couple) and its mission (the life between them results in new life from them). Marriage is not simply a relationship between two people but is also a relationship of creativity and service for others.

Heart of true love

Cardinal Basil Hume reminds us further that a healthy family is fundamentally at odds with our culture because it is radically anti-individualistic. He believed that taking the family responsibility seriously can lead people away from seeing themselves as the centre of the world, and to acknowledge the claims made by spouse, children and parents. He states that there is a kind of suffering love, struggle and sacrifice which every family will experience if it is to survive and grow strong. Indeed, is it not so that such an experience lies at the heart of true love.

The challenge

The challenge for teachers and parents in our Catholic schools is to teach, inform and encourage pupils to co-operate with God's plan for each one's wholeness and holiness and mentor them into responsible maturity.

Glossary

An aid for the teacher (What the Church teaches)

Abortion

Human life is so precious and unique that it must be respected and protected from the moment of conception. From this moment Christians have recognised the human being, that God is forming in the womb, as sacred and inviolable. Therefore the deliberate termination of a pregnancy, is gravely wrong.

Aids (Acquired Immune Deficiency Syndrome) is a physical condition caused by a virus, in which the body loses its ability to resist infection. Aids is transmitted by sexual intercourse, through infected blood, needles and blood products, and through the placenta. Regardless of whether the act by which the virus is transmitted is moral or immoral; the actual condition is neither. It is a tragic life threatening disease that deserves Christian compassion and care.

Annulment

For a Christian marriage to be genuine, that is valid and lawful, certain conditions apply. For example, each person who is marrying must be completely free to make the life-long commitment involved. If, after the marriage ceremony, one or more of the conditions can be proved to be unfulfilled, the Church authorities can be petitioned to declare that the marriage is not valid and can be declared null and void. There must be a serious reason and solid proof for such a petition.

Birth Control (see Contraception)

Celibacy

Making a conscious choice not to marry and abstain from sexual relationships is usually associated with the Catholic priesthood and the religious life, although it is a life style open to all. Consecrated celibacy ('for the sake of the Kingdom', Catechism of the Catholic Church 1579) is intended as a witness and sign of total dedication to Christ and his Church.

A Journey in Love

GLOSSARY

Chastity

Abstaining from sexual intercourse, until married, for example while preparing to marry, is a Christian virtue and considered one of the fruits of the Holy Spirit. (see Celibacy)

Conscience

The Church teaches (CCC 1778) that a person is bound to follow faithfully what he or she truly believes to be right and just.
This judgement, which needs to be informed, springs from the person's reason, which recognises the moral quality of an action that she/he is going to perform or has performed.

Contraception

Since the Church considers, for sound reasons, that the place for sexual intercourse is only within marriage, contraception is considered as the 'regulation of births,' for example, the spacing of births within the family. (CCC 2368). A distinction is made between natural and artificial means of contraception. Natural is the use of the infertile periods of the wife; artificial is the use of condoms, the pill, the cap etc. 'Natural', because it accords with Nature, is approved; artificial means are considered sinful.

(Catholic teaching does not allow any form of contraception outside marriage. It cannot support policies that encourage the use of contraceptives by young people to minimise teenage pregnancies.)

Dignity of the individual

Individual persons are consciously aware of their separate personal individuality; the Church would add, that being created by a loving God is the source of this individuality and dignity. It is from this that Human Rights spring.

Divorce

The marriage promises (vows) spell out the exclusive and permanent nature of the life-long marriage commitment. The Church believes that if mature persons freely choose to make such a commitment, and all the conditions for a valid marriage are present, it is a sacramental and unbreakable union. Divorce is a judgement of the courts of the civil authorities (the State) that the bond of marriage is declared broken or dissolved. It is a civil act not acknowledged by the Church; although pastors will do all they can to help and support divorced persons.

GLOSSARY

Family

Love, with its accompanying security, is the first basic need of the newborn child; this is best supplied and experienced in the unit of mother, father and child(ren) that we know as 'the family'.
This natural and traditional unit of society provides the balanced care of both female and male to promote the child's growth to autonomous and mature independence. In single parent families, that exist for whatever reason, the lone parent does his/her best to supply for the missing parent.

Homosexuality

Men and women who are sexually attracted to members of the same sex, prefer to be known as Gay or Lesbian. The Church upholds the dignity of every individual and utterly condemns any unjust discrimination or abuse directed against people who are homosexual; on the contrary they must be accepted with respect, compassion and sensitivity. Insofar as the homosexual orientation can lead to sexual activity which excludes openness to the generation of new human life and the essential sexual complementarity of man and woman, it is, in this particular and precise sense only, objectively disordered. However, it must be quite clear that a homosexual orientation must never be considered sinful or evil in itself.

Love of self

Christ gave us the twofold commandment, 'Love God with your whole heart... and your neighbour, as yourself' (Matthew 22:36-40). Jesus was very wise, because you cannot give to others what you do not possess; a healthy love of self must come first. This is simply defined as 'looking after ourselves, taking care of our bodies and minds and avoiding stress as much as possible' (Dr Jack Dominian). We cannot exaggerate our own worth; but this must be balanced by a truthful recognition that every person is unique and God-loved, otherwise love of self can become selfishness which fails to acknowledge and respect others.

Marriage

Love for another, of the opposite sex, compels the gift of oneself; marriage is that gift formalised by a life-long, exclusive commitment. The Church calls it in imitation of the loving friendship between God and his People, revealed in the Bible, a 'covenant', which forms an 'intimate community of life and love established by the Creator and endowed by him with its own proper laws: (CCC 1603) This covenant, which creates a bond between the couple, is one of the seven sacraments of the Church.

Masturbation

A mature and Christian understanding, of the intimate sexual relations in marriage, is that the word 'intercourse' is real and important.
In sexual union – love-making – the act is a sign that 'speaks' and expresses the love of the couple. In the most intimate of ways they make a gift of themselves to one another.
A life-bestowing act. Masturbation, however, is the expression of a lonely act, which is for the gratification of the individual.
While in childhood and adolescence it is commonly recognised as a natural part of growing up, its continuing into adulthood may be prompted by a complexity of reasons. The Church has always regarded it as a 'disordered action' (CCC 2352) but advises that moral responsibility for the act and pastoral action must take into account affective maturity; the force of an acquired habit; conditions of stress and anxiety or other psychological or social factors.

Premarital sex

The sign of the covenant of Marriage and also of the sacrament (see Marriage) is sexual intercourse. This is the deepest, most intimate and wonderful of all human signs; it is the 'language' of love. (It is called 'making love' and intercourse.) In teaching that sexual intercourse is reserved for marriage, the Church is protecting its dignity and worth; for it is the only way that God, who is Love, has decided to create a new human being. Our society has permitted and encouraged the debasement of this beautiful, life-enhancing act between a married couple and is currently reaping the consequences.

> "In the name of God, respect, protect, love and serve life, every human life"
>
> John Paul II in the Gospel of Life

'Love is an art to be learned.
It is a giving experience,
a selfless act.
Every experience of love
gives us yet another glimpse
of the meaning of love in God himself.
Human love is the instrument we can use
to explore the mystery of love
which God is.'

Cardinal Basil Hume